FREE STANDEES

ARE YOU A MEMBER OF THE ALLIANCE OR HORDE?

INSTRUCTIONS

1. Pull out the standee page.

2. Pop out the two standees and the four rectangle shapes.

3. Slot the rectangle pieces in to the slits on the standees to make the legs.

4. Choose your side. Alliance or Horde.

**BE CAREFUL WHEN USING SCISSORS.
ASK AN ADULT FOR HELP.**

CONTENTS

Pedigree®

Published 2014. Pedigree Books Limited, Beech Hill
House, Walnut Gardens, Exeter, Devon EX4 4DH.
www.pedigreebooks.com – books@pedigreegroup.co.uk
The Pedigree trademark, email and website addresses,
are the sole and exclusive properties of Pedigree
Group Limited, used under licence in this publication.

ACKNOWLEDGEMENTS
The publisher would like to thank the following:

Editorial: Anne Stickney

Design: Jonathan Finch

Licensing: Brian Mulcahy, Mike Hummel & Jerry Chu

Vault Team: Emily Mei, Leanne Huynh, Dana Bishop,
Steven Park, Joslyn Field & Roger Howard

ANVIL: Mike Bybee, Cate Gary, Sean Copeland,
Justin Parker & Joshua Horst

THE PEOPLE OF AZEROTH

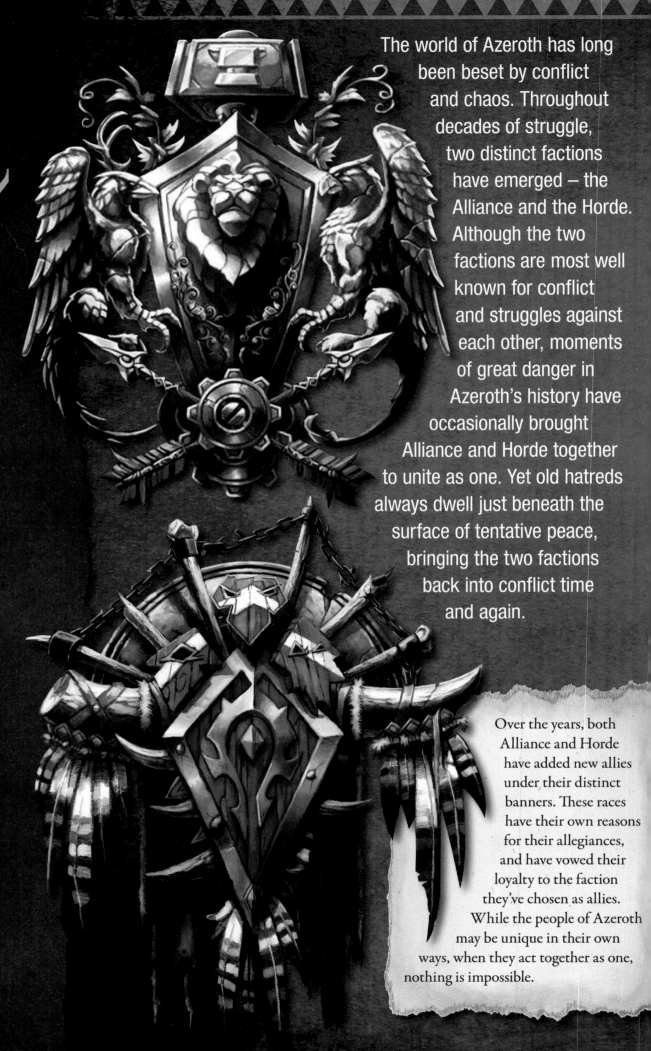

The world of Azeroth has long been beset by conflict and chaos. Throughout decades of struggle, two distinct factions have emerged – the Alliance and the Horde. Although the two factions are most well known for conflict and struggles against each other, moments of great danger in Azeroth's history have occasionally brought Alliance and Horde together to unite as one. Yet old hatreds always dwell just beneath the surface of tentative peace, bringing the two factions back into conflict time and again.

Over the years, both Alliance and Horde have added new allies under their distinct banners. These races have their own reasons for their allegiances, and have vowed their loyalty to the faction they've chosen as allies. While the people of Azeroth may be unique in their own ways, when they act together as one, nothing is impossible.

THE ALLIANCE

United in their goal, the noble races of the Alliance share an unwavering commitment to preserve order and protect Azeroth. Together, the united races of the Alliance stand as one, strong and proud against the forces of darkness that threaten the world.

HUMAN

The noble humans of Azeroth form the backbone of the Alliance. Led by the cunning warrior King Varian Wrynn, the human race stands as a beacon of fierce tenacity and unity in the face of adversity.

NIGHT ELF

An ancient race, the night elves, or kaldorei, have a history that spans back much further than their ties with the Alliance. Led by Tyrande Whisperwind and Malfurion Stormrage, the night elves offer centuries of untold wisdom and battle prowess to the Alliance.

DWARF

The hardy dwarves of the Alliance are led by the Council of Three Hammers. The council is composed of representatives from three dwarven clans – from the Bronzebeard clan, Muradin Bronzebeard; from the Wildhammer clan, Falstad Wildhammer; and from the Dark Iron clan, Moira Thaurissan.

GNOME

Masters of technological prowess, and staunch friends of the dwarven race, the gnomes of the Alliance are led by High Tinker Gelbin Mekkatorque.

DRAENEI

Forced to flee their homeworld of Argus when it was devoured by the Burning Legion, the noble draenei, led by the Prophet Velen, have traveled the universe for millennia. Eventually their travels brought them to Azeroth, where they joined forces with the Alliance.

WORGEN

The human kingdom of Gilneas withdrew from the world years ago, constructing a great wall to keep out troubles and threats. Yet a powerful curse was let loose on the proud kingdom, transforming many of its citizens into monstrous worgen. In the midst of struggles with the curse, the world itself shattered, letting enemies lay siege to the kingdom and forcing the Gilneans' hand. Now, the worgen, led by King Genn Greymane, have joined forces with the Alliance.

THE HORDE

The powerful Horde once began as an invasion force largely composed of orc clans, but it has since grown into far more. A family of disparate races, the Horde stands united to fight for survival and prosperity in an unfriendly world.

ORC

Strength and honor drive the orcs, a powerful race that originally hailed from the distant world of Draenor. Although their history has been fraught with conflict, the orcs have united and embraced their freedom on Azeroth, brought together by their former warchief Thrall.

TROLL

Once part of the mighty troll empires of old, the Darkspear tribe of trolls found itself cast out by its kin. Taken under the wing of the Horde by Warchief Thrall, the Darkspears have since not only survived, but triumphed – their leader, Chieftain Vol'jin, now leads as warchief of the Horde as well.

TAUREN

A noble race that embraces the natural world, the tauren have shed their nomadic roots and united in their ancestral lands. Led by High Chieftain Baine Bloodhoof, the tauren provide both strength and wisdom to the Horde.

FORSAKEN

The undead Forsaken were once part of the mindless Scourge that razed the former human kingdom of Lordaeron. After breaking free of the domination of their dark master, the Forsaken were united by their leader, the Banshee Queen, Sylvanas Windrunner. Although their dark past may be cause for uneasy suspicion, none in the Horde can deny that the Forsaken are powerful allies.

BLOOD ELF

The high elves of Quel'Thalas were nearly wiped out by the Scourge during the Third War. In remembrance of the fallen, the beleaguered race took the name sin'dorei, or blood elves. Betrayed by the Alliance, the sin'dorei were forced to seek refuge elsewhere, and found it with the Horde. Led by Regent Lord Lor'themar Theron, the blood elves tenaciously fight to restore their nation's glory.

GOBLIN

The shrewd, cunning goblins of the Bilgewater Cartel were once a neutral group that lived on the remote island of Kezan. After the world was shattered during the Cataclysm, the goblins were forced to flee. Although betrayed and imprisoned by their leader, Trade Prince Jastor Gallywix, the goblins found their salvation with the former warchief of the Horde, Thrall. No longer neutral, the Bilgewater Cartel now sides with the Horde, offering ingenious inventions ... for the right price, of course.

THE PANDAREN

The pandaren of the Wandering Isle spent countless centuries travelling the seas of Azeroth on the back of the Great Turtle, Shen-zin Su, seeking nothing more than a quiet life of tranquil peace. Yet recent events drew the pandaren of the Wandering Isle into joining the conflict between Alliance and Horde, after an Alliance ship carrying Horde prisoners crashed into Shen-zin Su. From that first tentative contact with the outside world, the residents of the Wandering Isle were given a unique opportunity. Rather than side with one faction over the other, each individual pandaren was allowed to choose whether to join Alliance or Horde, and experience all that each faction had to offer.

Instead of a racial leader, the pandaren have two diplomatic representatives, one for each faction. Aysa Cloudsinger decided to follow the Alliance, while Ji Firepaw chose to follow the Horde.

FACTION CROSSWORD

How well do you know your races and factions? Put your brain to the test and solve the questions to fill in the crossword!

ACROSS

1. Former orc warchief of the Horde.
6. Aysa _____ is the pandaren diplomatic representative to the Alliance.
7. The worgen are led by King Genn _____.
8. Sylvanas Windrunner is known as the _____ Queen.
9. High Chieftain Baine _____ leads the tauren.
10. King _____ Wrynn leads the humans of the Alliance.
13. The goblins of the _____ Cartel joined the Horde.
14. The three dwarven clans are represented by three dwarven leaders, Muradin Bronzebeard, Falstad Wildhammer, and Moira _____.
17. The undead _____ were once part of the mindless Scourge, but now ally with the Horde.
19. The gnomes are led by High Tinker Gelbin _____.
21. One of the night elf leaders is _____ Whisperwind.
22. This faction seeks to preserve order and protect Azeroth.
23. The draenei are led by the _____ Velen.
24. The shrewd, cunning goblins that have allied with the Horde once lived on this remote island.
25. The worgen were originally humans from this kingdom.
26. The high elves were nearly wiped out by the Scourge during the _____ War.
27. The Great Turtle, which carried the pandaren over the oceans of Azeroth, is also referred to as the _____ Isle.
29. This faction once began as an invasion force.
30. This troll chieftain now leads as warchief of the Horde.

DOWN

2. The dwarves of the Alliance are led by the Council of Three _____.
3. Once nomadic, the tauren have since united in their _____ lands.
4. The high elves of _____ now call themselves blood elves in remembrance of those who were wiped out by Scourge during the Third War.
5. Friends of the dwarves, gnomes are also known for being masters of _____ prowess.
11. Another name for night elves.
12. The troll tribe that joined the Horde.
15. The other leader of the night elves is named Malfurion _____.
16. The blood elves are led by Regent Lord _____ Theron.
18. Pandaren that have since joined either Alliance or Horde once traveled the seas of Azeroth on the back of the Great Turtle, _____-____ Su.
20. Goblins that have allied with the Horde are led by Trade Prince Jastor _____.
28. The orcs originally hailed from the distant world of _____.

CHOOSE YOUR FACTION

ARE YOU A VALIANT PROTECTOR OF THE ALLIANCE, OR A STALWART WARRIOR OF THE HORDE? CHOOSE YOUR SIDE, THEN COLLECT EVERYTHING YOU'LL NEED TO DESIGN YOUR OWN T-SHIRT.

1. SCAN OR PHOTOCOPY THE SYMBOLS ON THE OPPOSITE PAGE TO CREATE YOUR STENCIL.

2. USING A CRAFT KNIFE OR SCISSORS, CAREFULLY CUT OUT ALL THE BLACK AREAS TO MAKE THE STENCIL HOLES.

3. TAPE YOUR STENCIL TO THE CARD USING MASKING TAPE THEN CUT OUT A STRONGER STENCIL FROM THE CARD.

4. USE MASKING TAPE TO ATTACH THE STENCIL TO THE FRONT OF YOUR T-SHIRT.

5. PAINT THROUGH THE STENCIL ONTO YOUR T-SHIRT MAKING SURE YOU COVER ALL THE HOLES.

6. SLOWLY AND GENTLY PEEL AWAY THE STENCIL, THEN WAIT FOR THE PAINT TO DRY.

7. IF YOUR PAINT NEEDS TO BE FIXED USING AN IRON, FOLLOW THE INSTRUCTIONS ON THE PACKET. COVER THE PAINT WITH A CLOTH TO STOP IT STICKING TO THE IRON.

ASK AN ADULT TO HELP YOU WHEN USING SCISSORS AND AN IRON.

TRAVEL GUIDE AND MAPS

KALIMDOR

Kalimdor is located on the western half of Azeroth. Primarily known for being the home of the night elves, Kalimdor has several races that call its shores home. The orcish race resides in the deserts of Durotar, and just north lies the region of Azshara, which the Bilgewater Cartel of goblins have claimed as their new home. The once-nomadic tauren have since settled in the verdant central grasslands of Mulgore. In addition, the trolls of the Darkspear tribe have settled on the southern shores of Durotar and claimed the Echo Isles, and the draenei have settled on Azuremyst Isle off the northwestern coast near Teldrassil, the World Tree that is the primary home of the night elves and, after the Cataclysm, the Gilnean refugees, including the worgen.

EASTERN KINGDOMS

The Eastern Kingdoms are known as the primary home of the human race, who covered much of the land in the earlier years of Azeroth's history. The ravages of war have taken their toll on the land and shifted the various human settlements. Now the human race primarily resides in Stormwind and the surrounding areas, while the dwarves and gnomes populate the snowy reaches of Khaz Modan. To the north, the Forsaken have claimed much of the region formerly known as the kingdom of Lordaeron, and in the distant northeast, the blood elves reside in the forests of Quel'Thalas.

PANDARIA

Shrouded in dense mists over ten thousand years ago, the southern continent of Pandaria was nothing more than legend until the mists recently parted and revealed the continent to Azeroth's explorers. Once tranquil and serene, much of Pandaria was affected when the war between the Alliance and Horde reached its shores. The lush jungles of the Jade Forest lie along the eastern coast, while the western coast contains the Dread Wastes, ravaged wasteland of the insectoid mantid, and the Townlong Steppes. The Krasarang Wilds along the southern coast should be traveled with caution, and the highest peaks of Pandaria's mountains lie in Kun-Lai Summit to the north. Pandaria's heartland includes the Valley of the Four Winds, the continent's agricultural hub, and the mysterious Vale of Eternal Blossoms, only recently revealed to travelers both Alliance and Horde.

NORTHREND

The icy continent of Northrend is dotted with titan facilities like those found in the inexplicably tropical Sholazar Basin, and the titan complex Ulduar, located in the Storm Peaks. At the heart of Northrend is the Dragonblight, final resting place for Azeroth's dragons. Other regions include the southern reaches of Howling Fjord and Borean Tundra, as well as the forests of Grizzly Hills, and the troll wasteland of Zul'Drak. Although many creatures co-exist on the continent, it is best known for holding the most concentrated population of undead Scourge, as well as the Lich King, who sits upon the Frozen Throne in Icecrown.

TRAVEL GUIDE AND MAPS

The shattered realm of Outland is a harsh, bleak remnant of the world once called Draenor, destroyed by clashing cataclysmic energies from a series of gateways to other worlds. The unforgiving red sands of Hellfire Peninsula are home to orcs twisted by fel magic, while the swamps of Zangarmarsh lie to the west, overrun by naga. To the north, the jagged spires of Blade's Edge Mountains are home of both ogre and monstrous gronn. The upper reaches of Netherstorm contain chaotic magics harnessed by manaforges, dotted by great eco-domes containing the last of Netherstorm's greenery, carefully cultivated by the ethereals.

OUTLAND

NETHERSTORM

BLADE'S EDGE MOUNTAINS

ZANGARMARSH

HELLFIRE PENINSULA

NAGRAND

TEROKKAR FOREST

SHADOWMOON VALLEY

OUTLAND

To the southwest, the region of Nagrand remains verdant, almost untouched by fel energies - but the fiery wasteland of Shadowmoon Valley to the southeast is a chaotic storm of fel magic and demonic intrusion, home to the foul Black Temple. Nestled between the two regions is Terokkar Forest, most notably the location of both the haunted subterranean ruins of Auchindoun, and Shattrath City, a sanctuary city that takes in travelers from all regions of the world.

DRAENOR

Prior to the creation of Outland, Draenor was a land of magma and metal, stone and steam. Home to both savage orc and enigmatic draenei, Draenor is also host to a variety of exotic and dangerous creatures, both fauna and flora alike. To the north, the once-glistening oasis of Gorgrond lies a desolate, rocky badland of steam vents that boil from deep beneath the earth. In the northwest, Frostfire Ridge is a harsh land of ceaseless winter and volcanic peaks. Across the Sea of Zangar, the windswept plains of Nagrand hold veiled threats of their own, and at the heart of the continent rests Talador, divided by rivers that flow from the Sea of Zangar.

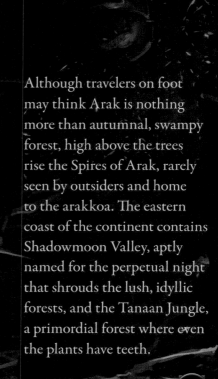

Although travelers on foot may think Arak is nothing more than autumnal, swampy forest, high above the trees rise the Spires of Arak, rarely seen by outsiders and home to the arakkoa. The eastern coast of the continent contains Shadowmoon Valley, aptly named for the perpetual night that shrouds the lush, idyllic forests, and the Tanaan Jungle, a primordial forest where even the plants have teeth.

21

ALLIANCE CAPITALS

STORMWIND CITY

REGION: Eastern Kingdoms   **RACE:** Human

Stormwind City is the human capital. The city was besieged by the mighty dragon Deathwing during the Cataclysm, and work still continues on repairing the damage. Stormwind Keep is home to King Varian Wrynn and the royal court.

IRONFORGE

REGION: Eastern Kingdoms
RACE: Dwarf

Ironforge is the great dwarven capital city, carved into the heart of the mountains of Khaz Modan. Three dwarf clans reside in its stout walls – Bronzebeard, Wildhammer, and Dark Iron. Muradin Bronzebeard, Falstad Wildhammer, and Moira Thaurissan lead the three clans jointly, forming the Council of Three Hammers.

DARNASSUS

REGION: Kalimdor

RACE: Night Elf / Worgen

High atop the branches of the World Tree Teldrassil lies the night elf capital of Darnassus. The Temple of the Moon on the southern side of the city is home to both Tyrande Whisperwind and Malfurion Stormrage, who jointly lead the night elf race. Also located in Darnassus is the Howling Oak, home and shelter to displaced Gilnean worgen.

GNOMEREGAN

REGION: Eastern Kingdoms
RACE: Gnome

The subterranean city of Gnomeregan was thought lost to the gnomish race, but recent efforts have seen some success in reclaiming the capital. Led by High Tinker Gelbin Mekkatorque, the gnomes of Azeroth are still hard at work to reclaim their home, staging their efforts from the outpost of New Tinkertown.

EXODAR

REGION: Kalimdor

RACE: Draenei

Once a wing of the dimensional ship known as Tempest Keep, the *Exodar* was used by the draenei to flee Outland. Blood elf saboteurs caused the ship to crash into Azeroth's seas, stranding the draenei on Azuremyst Isle. Although it was damaged in the fall, the *Exodar* has since been repaired, its crystalline halls ready for flight if the Prophet Velen, leader of the draenei, deems it necessary.

ORGRIMMAR

REGION: Kalimdor

RACE: Orc

Nearly destroyed in the Cataclysm, the orcish capital of Orgrimmar was rebuilt by former warchief Garrosh Hellscream into a bristling citadel of iron and strength. Although Orgrimmar is primarily the orc capital, its sprawling canyons hold valleys that host troll, tauren, and goblin settlers as well.

UNDERCITY

REGION: Eastern Kingdoms
RACE: Forsaken

Hidden beneath the ruined capital city of Lordaeron, the Undercity, once a series of catacombs, sewers, and dungeons, is now the home of the Forsaken. The Banshee Queen, Sylvanas Windrunner, leads her people from the well-guarded depths of the Royal Quarter.

DARKSPEAR ISLE

REGION: Kalimdor

RACE: Troll

Darkspear Isle and the surrounding Echo Isles were once thought lost to the trolls, but clever planning by their leader, Chieftain Vol'jin, led to their reclamation. Now the Darkspears once again call the islands home, although Vol'jin leads not just the Darkspears but the Horde itself as warchief.

SILVERMOON CITY

REGION: Eastern Kingdoms
RACE: Blood Elf

Although the shining capital city of the blood elves was dealt a devastating blow when the Scourge invaded, Silvermoon City was restored and now stands as a thriving capital. Led by Regent Lord Lor'themar Theron, the blood elves still work to scour the last remnants of the Scourge from the surrounding forests of Quel'Thalas.

THUNDER BLUFF

REGION: Kalimdor

RACE: Tauren

High atop great rises in the tauren ancestral lands of Mulgore lies the tauren capital of Thunder Bluff. Only accessible from the valley below by two great lifts, the rise is easily defended by capable tauren warriors. High Chieftain Baine Bloodhoof leads the tauren from Central Rise.

CAPITAL

STORMWIND

ORGRIMMAR

THUNDER BLUFF

GILNEAS

DWARF

HOME
CITY: ....

ORC

HOME
CITY: ....

FORSAKEN

HOME
CITY: ....

BLOOD ELF

HOME
CITY: ....

MATCH-UP

Help each character find their home city!

SILVERMOON CITY

EXODAR

IRONFORGE

UNDERCITY

HUMAN
HOME CITY: ....

TAUREN
HOME CITY: ....

WORGEN
HOME CITY: ....

DRAENEI
HOME CITY: ....

Did you match them all? Check your answers on page 76.

GNOME vs GOBLIN

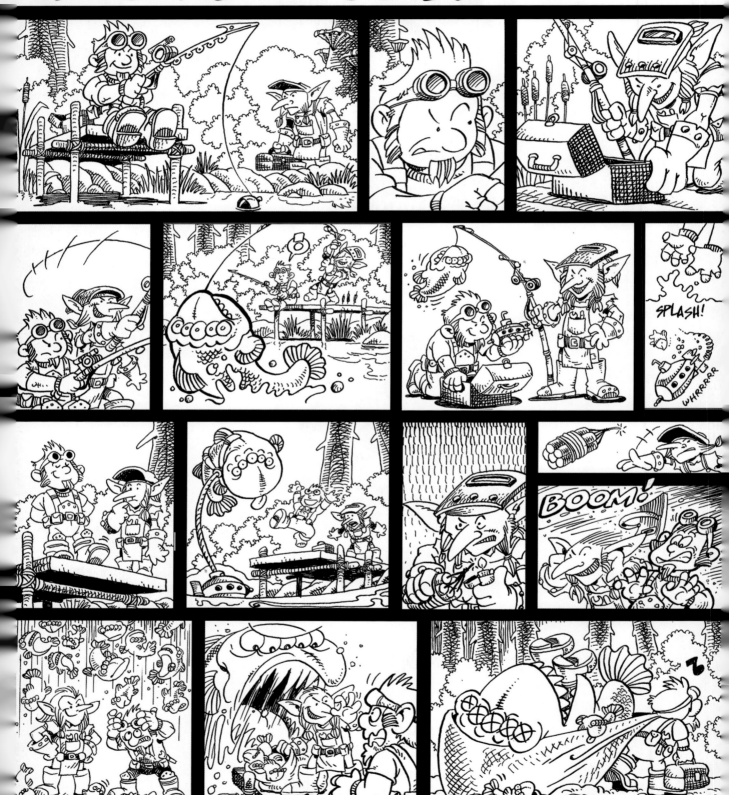

GNOME vs GOBLIN

"Slow and steady wins the race!" | Story by Micky Neilson & James Waugh | Art by Stan Sakai

GNOME vs GOBLIN

KABLAM!

BOOM!

PET BATTLES

Azeroth is home to a variety of creatures, some large and threatening, some very small. Heroes traveling the world can collect pets to call their own. But Azeroth's smallest denizens are just as fierce as the monsters that face champions of the world in epic battles. With the Pet Battle system, players can capture wild pets, train them to grow stronger, create teams for battling, and even pit their pets against other players.

Battle Pets come in ten different families, each with its own unique strengths and weaknesses. A clever trainer will want to keep these strengths and weaknesses in mind when creating a team.

ELEMENTAL

Strong against Mechanical pets, but weak against Aquatic pets. Elementals ignore all negative weather effects.

FLYING

Strong against Beast pets, but weak against Magic pets. Flying creatures have a 50% boost to speed while above 50% health.

AQUATIC

Strong against Undead pets, but weak against Flying pets. Aquatic pets take 50% less damage from damage over time abilities.

HUMANOID

Strong against Critter pets, but weak against Undead pets. Humanoids recover 5% of their maximum health with every attack.

BEAST

Strong against Humanoid pets, but weak against Mechanical pets. Beast pets deal 25% extra damage when below half health.

MAGIC

Strong against Aquatic pets, but weak against Dragonkin pets. Magic pets cannot be dealt damage greater than 35% of their maximum health in a single attack.

CRITTER

Strong against Elemental pets, but weak against Beast pets. Critters are wily, and immune to stun, root, and sleep effects.

MECHANICAL

Strong against Magic pets, but weak against Elemental pets. Mechanical pets will come back to life once per battle, with 25% health.

DRAGONKIN

Strong against Flying pets, but weak against Humanoid pets. Dragons deal 50% more damage on the next round, after they bring their opponent below 50% health.

UNDEAD

Strong against Dragonkin pets, but weak against Critter pets. Undead pets return to life when killed, immortal for one round.

CAPTURING PETS

Every pet in Azeroth has a unique set of abilities it can use in combat. Wild pets that can be captured will have a green paw icon over their heads. Engage the pet in battle, and once your team has taken it below 35% health, you can try throwing a trap at it. Successfully trap the pet, and it will automatically be added to your collection at the end of the battle.

CHALLENGING BATTLES

Special pet tamers are scattered all over Azeroth, waiting for up-and-coming teams to challenge them in battle. Most tamers have very strong pets, and require clever thinking and strategy to defeat. In Pandaria, the legendary Beasts of Fable await. Only the strongest teams can defeat these mysterious beasts of legend. And on the Timeless Isle, the Celestial Tournament is a battle of wits, pitting the most veteran Pet Battle champions against some of Pandaria's most notable characters.

MOUNTS
OF THE
ALLIANCE AND HORDE

Traveling through Azeroth and beyond is often difficult and fraught with peril. While various factions have established flight paths between distant locations, adventurous heroes also have the option of obtaining various steeds. Each race in the Alliance and Horde has its own unique racial mount to ride, and heroes who have earned a favorable reputation among these races can obtain a steed of their own.

ALLIANCE

RACE: **HUMAN**
MOUNT: **HORSE**

RACE: **GNOME**
MOUNT: **MECHANOSTRIDER**

RACE: **DWARF**   MOUNT: **RAM**

RACE: **DRAENEI**
MOUNT: **ELEKK**

RACE: **NIGHT ELF**
MOUNT: **NIGHTSABER**

HORDE

RACE: **BLOOD ELF**
MOUNT: **HAWKSTRIDER**

RACE: **PANDAREN**
MOUNT: **DRAGON TURTLE**

RACE: **TAUREN**
MOUNT: **KODO**

RACE: **GOBLIN**
MOUNT: **TRIKE**

RACE: **FORSAKEN**
MOUNT: **SKELETAL HORSE**

RACE: **TROLL**
MOUNT: **RAPTOR**

RACE: **ORC** MOUNT: **WOLF**

LEGENDARY ITEMS
WEAPONS OF LEGEND

Azeroth's heroes may be strong, but they cannot defeat the forces of darkness with bravery and strength alone. Over the years, weapons of great power have been revealed. These legendary weapons are difficult to obtain, but the powers they possess are worth the journey it takes to obtain them.

SULFURAS, HAND OF RAGNAROS

This mighty hammer is the legendary weapon of Ragnaros the Firelord. Ragnaros ruled from the Firelands, elemental plane of fire. For a time, Ragnaros was bound to the depths of Molten Core, and those brave enough to defeat him could obtain the means to forge this legendary weapon.

THUNDERFURY, BLESSED BLADE OF THE WINDSEEKER

Thunderaan, Prince of Air, once wielded this blade, but he was defeated by Ragnaros. He then forced Thunderaan's essence into a talisman, shattering it and giving the two halves to his lieutenants, Garr and Baron Geddon. Although Thunderaan could never be released, the blade served as a vessel for his essence, a powerful weapon graced with the fury of the storm.

THORI'DAL, THE STARS' FURY

This legendary bow resonates with the power of the Sunwell, a magical font of energy created by the high elves. Although the origins and history of the weapon remain a mystery, it can still be found at the site of the Sunwell, on the Isle of Quel'Danas. Those seeking the weapon will first have to defeat the eredar demon lord Kil'jaeden.

THE TWIN BLADES OF AZZINOTH

A pair of fel green warglaives, the Twin Blades of Azzinoth are wielded by Illidan Stormrage, self-proclaimed lord of Outland. The twin brother of Malfurion Stormrage, Illidan was imprisoned for 10,000 years, and later banished from night elf civilization entirely. Now Illidan leads his forces from the haunted halls of the Black Temple, his glaives waiting to be claimed by those with the strength to best him in combat.

VALANYR, HAMMER OF ANCIENT KINGS

Created by the titans, the hammer Val'anyr was given to Urel Stoneheart, the first king of the earthen race. The weapon was shattered during the first war between the earthen and the iron dwarves. Although the fragments were believed to be lost, heroes can still find them in the depths of the titan stronghold of Ulduar, if willing to brave the might of the Old God Yogg-Saron.

DRAGONWRATH, TARECGOSA'S REST

After the death of Malygos, Aspect of the blue dragonflight, a new leader had to be chosen. Yet corruption ran rampant through the blue dragons, and it was through Tarecgosa's sacrifice that the culprits were revealed. Now, Tarecgosa's spirit lives on in Dragonwrath, bound to it for eternity.

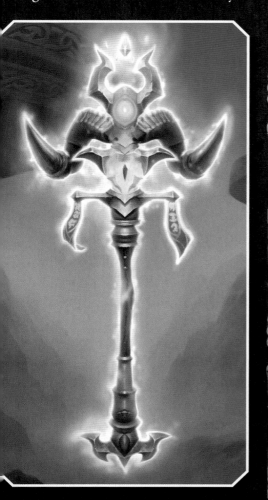

SHADOWMOURNE

The legendary axe Shadowmourne is a new creation, one forged from the hardened blood of the Old God Yogg-Saron, and drenched in the souls of the dead. Highlord Darion Mograine came up with the idea to create the weapon as a hopeful counterpoint to Frostmourne, the blade wielded by the Lich King. With Shadowmourne, Mograine hoped that the war against the Lich King could at last be ended.

FANGS OF THE FATHER

These vicious twin daggers were created by Wrathion as a reward for assisting him in the dubious task of taking out his own kind. Newly hatched, Wrathion wished to extinguish the last of his corrupted dragonflight, leaving him as the sole, uncorrupted survivor. In order to complete this grave task, heroes had to pass a series of trials that ended with the killing of Wrathion's father, Deathwing.

A LEGEND
IN THE MAKING

After the Cataclysm, the black dragon Wrathion was, to his knowledge, the only one left of his kind. Free from the corruption of the Old Gods, Wrathion traveled to Pandaria after experiencing a vision of Azeroth's destruction. To combat the threat, Wrathion would need a united army. To that end, Wrathion sought out the bravest of heroes for a unique journey that would take them from the halls of mogu emperors to the seat of the Horde warchief, collecting valuable rewards along the way.

TRIAL OF THE BLACK PRINCE

In the first leg of Wrathion's journey, heroes had to collect sigils of power and wisdom from the foes that threatened Pandaria. Once the horrors of the mogu and mantid were vanquished, those with the strength to carry on were asked to bring back the very essence of fear itself from the dread Sha of Fear. Satisfied with the progress made, Wrathion took the power and wisdom of foes vanquished, combined it with the essence of fear conquered, and created Crystallized Gems to augment the powers of any sha-touched weapon.

WRATHION'S WAR

Yet Wrathion's tasks were far from over, and with the arrival of Alliance and Horde fleets upon Pandaria's shores, the black dragon had a new task - to swiftly end the war between the two factions. For Wrathion, the victor in the war mattered little, so long as the two factions were as one in the end of the struggle. The purpose was a united front to face the horrors in Wrathion's vision. And heroes that diligently completed Wrathion's tasks were richly rewarded with the Eye of the Black Prince, which would add an additional socket to their weapons.

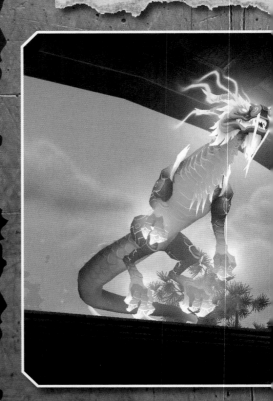

TWO PRINCES

In search of more power, Wrathion sought the secrets of the lost mogu empire of Lei Shen, the Thunder King, when Lei Shen was reborn. Yet his motives were brought into question by the human Prince Anduin Wrynn. As Wrathion continued to delve into the mystery of the mogu, uncovering their connection to the titans along the way, Anduin remained suspicious. Even so, heroes that completed Wrathion's tasks were richly rewarded with the Crown of Heaven, a magically enhanced gem that would allow the eyes of Wrathion to see through the helm of whoever wore it.

JUDGMENT OF THE BLACK PRINCE

Wrathion's curiosity was born anew with the sudden appearance of the Timeless Isle off the coast of Pandaria. Adrift in the Sands of Time, the isle was also a haven for the August Celestials. Wrathion's final task set heroes to defeat each of the four celestials in turn. Once the task was completed, heroes were rewarded with a legendary cloak imbued with the powers of the celestials. Yet this was not the end of the journey – one final task remained. The war between Alliance and Horde came to a head in the Horde capital of Orgrimmar. Alliance forces were not alone in their battle – Horde rebels born as a result of Warchief Garrosh Hellscream's reckless leadership of the Horde joined the Alliance to strike. Yet Wrathion's vision of both factions ruled as one did not come to pass. After Hellscream's defeat, King Varian Wrynn left the rest of the Horde to rebuild. Furious, Wrathion departed Pandaria for good, vowing to prepare the world for the battle to come.

CELESTIAL BLESSINGS

While the heroes that had diligently completed Wrathion's tasks were well rewarded, they were still not as powerful as the black dragon would like. To that end, he sought out the four August Celestials of Pandaria, powerful guardians with unique powers all of their own. From each, he asked for a blessing. The celestials were not willing to give their blessing without a trial, however – a trial that would test the mettle of both the Black Prince, and the heroes that stood staunch at his side. The blessings were combined to create a powerful cloak to shield Wrathion's chosen, and augment their strength as well.

Wrathion would like to reward you for your heroic deeds!
But before he can do so, you must meet the challenge
of the August Celestials and defeat them in combat.
Find Yu'lon, Chi-Ji, Xuen, and Niuzao, then journey to
the Seat of Knowledge for your well-earned reward!

START

EMPEROR'S WAY

Each of the August Celestials embodies a different virtue. These virtues are reflected in the legendary cloaks that heroes can earn.

JINA-KANG, KINDNESS OF CHI-JI

Chi-Ji is also known as the Red Crane. His message of hope inspires the citizens of Pandaria, and his essence helps those who seek to heal their allies.

XING-HO, BREATH OF YU'LON

Yu'lon is also known as the Jade Serpent, incarnation of wisdom. Her teachings have long been hailed for their wisdom, and her essence helps those who choose to cast spells to damage their enemies.

GONG-LU, STRENGTH OF XUEN / FEN-YU, FURY OF XUEN

Xuen, also called the White Tiger, is the embodiment of strength. His essence provides those who would stand in the face of any danger with the strength to persevere.

QIAN-YING, FORTITUDE OF NIUZAO / QIAN-LE, COURAGE OF NIUZAO

The great Black Ox, Niuzao is the patron spirit of fortitude. He is the only celestial to choose to live beyond the wall, and his essence helps to shield those who would choose to defend and protect their allies.

WARCRAFT

SAGA

chapter one

STORIES by
CHRIS METZEN

ART by
ALEX HORLEY

SCRIPTING by
JAMES WAUGH

IT IS SAID THAT IN THE BEGINNING THERE WAS LIGHT AND THERE WAS VOID AND IN A TIME LONG AGO, THE TWO COLLIDED IN THE ABYSS OF THE GREAT DARK.

INFINITE WORLDS SPIRALED OUT INTO
THE NEWLY FORMING COSMOS....WORLDS
THAT WOULD ONE DAY BEAR LIFE FORMS
OF WONDROUS AND TERRIBLE DIVERSITY.

IN TIME, POWERFUL BEINGS AROSE AND SET
ABOUT BRINGING ORDER AND SHAPE TO THE
NASCENT UNIVERSE. THESE COLOSSAL ENTITIES
WERE KNOWN AS...

THE TITANS

UNFATHOMABLE TO MORTAL MINDS, THE TRUTH OF THESE GREAT GALACTIC BEINGS HAS LONG BEEN LOST AS WHISPERS BEGAT LEGENDS AND LEGENDS TURNED TO MYTH.

RULING OVER THE TITANS WAS AN ELITE SECT KNOWN AS THE PANTHEON...

- LEFT TO RIGHT -

NORGANNON
THE DREAMWEAVER, KEEPER OF CELESTIAL MAGICS AND LORE.

VKHAZ'GOROTH
THE SHAPER, FORGER OF WORLDS.

GOLGANNETH
THE THUNDERER, LORD OF THE SKIES AND ROARING OCEANS.

EONAR
THE LIFEBINDER, GENTLE CARETAKER OF ALL LIVING THINGS.

AGGRAMAR
THE AVENGER, LIEUTENANT OF THE GREAT SARGERAS.

AMAN'THUL
THE HIGHFATHER OF THE PANTHEON.

SARGERAS
THE DEFENDER, NOBLEST OF ALL.

DURING THE FIRST AGES OF CREATION, THE TITANS EXPLORED THE NEWBORN UNIVERSE.

THEY CRAFTED WORLDS OF INFINITE BEAUTY... RAISING MASSIVE MOUNTAINS AND DREDGING VAST SEAS. THEY BREATHED SKIES AND RAGING ATMOSPHERES INTO BEING.

FINALLY, THE PANTHEON EMPOWERED PRIMITIVE RACES TO TEND TO ITS WORKS AND MAINTAIN THE INTEGRITY OF THEIR RESPECTIVE WORLDS. THE FUTURE SEEMED BRIGHT. ASSURED. YET A GREAT SHADOW LOOMED....

FROM AN ETHEREAL DIMENSION OF WARRING MAGICS, KNOWN AS THE TWISTING NETHER, CAME LEGIONS OF RAVENOUS DEMONIC BEINGS.

THESE DEMONS HAD BUT ONE MALEVOLENT PURPOSE: TO DESTROY LIFE AND DEVOUR THE ENERGIES OF THE LIVING UNIVERSE.

SARGERAS, CHAMPION OF THE TITANS, WAS ELECTED TO HUNT DOWN THE DEMONIC ARMIES. HE CARRIED OUT HIS DUTY PROUDLY AND VOWED NEVER TO REST UNTIL THE DEMONS' EVIL BLIGHT HAD BEEN ERADICATED FROM EXISTENCE.

REGARDLESS, NO MATTER HOW HARD SARGERAS FOUGHT, THE MULTITUDES WOULD NOT RELENT, MADDENINGLY RAZING TEN WORLDS TO EVERY ONE WRESTLED FROM THEIR GRASP.

YET, THE DEMONS' GREATEST VICTORY WAS STILL TO COME...

SARGERAS, MOST HERALDED OF ALL TITANS, COULD NO LONGER BEAR THE HARSH TRUTH THAT, WHEREVER HE TURNED, EVIL AND DEPRAVITY SATURATED THE WHOLE OF CREATION.

HE CEASED THE FUTILITY OF HIS WAR AND JOINED THE VERY DEMONIC ARMIES HE ONCE HAD STRIVEN TO ANNIHILATE. NOW, HE LEADS THE FORCES OF WHAT IS KNOWN AS...

THE BURNING LEGION

AS THEY RAGE ACROSS THE STARS, SEEKING OUT WORLDS TO DESTROY AND THE VERY NOBLEST OF HEARTS TO CORRUPT...

UNTIL ALL THE UNIVERSE IS UNDONE.

THE HISTORY

The Warcraft franchise and the history of Azeroth began with a series of real-time strategy games. 2014 marked both the 10-year anniversary of *World of Warcraft*, and the 20-year anniversary of the Warcraft franchise itself. Warcraft received critical acclaim for both its engaging gameplay, and the intriguing story that played out over the course of the series, introducing beloved heroes and villains alike. The struggles of Azeroth and its shining heroes against monstrous forces of evil like the Burning Legion and the Scourge captured the imaginations of players all over the world.

WARCRAFT:
ORCS & HUMANS

For millennia, the fallen titan Sargeras sought to extinguish all life from the fragile world of Azeroth, to no avail. In an attempt to accomplish this task, Sargeras possessed the human sorcerer Medivh, compelling him to contact the orcish race that populated the distant world of Draenor. There, the Burning Legion had already taken its toll, and the bloodthirsty, relentless orc army known as the Horde roamed without purpose. Medivh and the orc warlock Gul'dan constructed a gateway between the two worlds known as the Dark Portal. With the gateway open, the monstrous armies of the Horde rushed through and struck, beginning the First War. Although Medivh was eventually defeated, the human kingdom of Stormwind was unable to withstand the might of the Horde's forces. The First War ended with Stormwind's crushing defeat.

OF WARCRAFT

WARCRAFT II: TIDES OF DARKNESS

Led by Anduin Lothar, the human survivors of the First War fled across the Great Sea to the kingdom of Lordaeron. King Terenas Menethil II heeded the warning of Lothar, and formed an alliance of some of Azeroth's races – human, dwarf, gnome, and high elf – to create the Alliance of Lordaeron. This mighty, united army sought to put an end to the Horde. Meanwhile, the Horde dealt with troubles from within. On the eve of what might have been the Horde's victory, Gul'dan and his followers abandoned the Horde's leader, Orgrim Doomhammer. In a harrowing battle, the Horde thought they had achieved victory when Doomhammer slew Anduin Lothar – but Lothar's death did little to sway the Alliance's resolve. Rallying around Lothar's lieutenant, the heroic paladin Turalyon, the Alliance armies quickly pulled together and dealt the Horde a crushing defeat, ending the Second War.

WARCRAFT II: BEYOND THE DARK PORTAL

On Azeroth, the Dark Portal was destroyed. Meanwhile on Draenor, an orc named Ner'zhul rose to command the remnants of the shattered Horde. Ner'zhul plotted to open portals to other worlds for the bloodthirsty Horde to invade. In order to accomplish this task, Ner'zhul sent forces through the Dark Portal to seek out powerful artifacts on Azeroth. In response, the Alliance Expedition was formed, and traveled through what remained of the Dark Portal to Draenor. Despite the Expedition's heroic efforts, Ner'zhul succeeded in opening countless portals to new worlds ripe for conquest. Yet Ner'zhul's efforts were in vain – the energies of the portals strained Draenor to its breaking point. Draenor shattered from the magical stress, stranding the Alliance Expedition on its remains, now called Outland.

WARCRAFT III:
REIGN OF CHAOS

In the years following the Second War, the last remnants of the once-mighty Horde struggled to survive in Alliance internment camps. Raised entirely in human captivity, one extraordinary orc named Thrall managed to escape, learning the ways of his people, and the ways of the shaman as well. He rallied together those orcs that had managed to elude capture and liberated the rest of the orcish race from their captivity, forming a new Horde. Yet Azeroth was under peril from a different, familiar source, as the armies of the Burning Legion sought to conquer the world once more. This time, the Legion unleashed a new, horrifying weapon to weaken the world's defenses – the undead Scourge.

The human Prince Arthas Menethil of Lordaeron fought valiantly to end the undead threat, yet he soon found himself falling into darkness, joining forces with the Lich King, the monstrous leader of the Scourge. Meanwhile, Thrall's new Horde set sail for the continent of Kalimdor, finding new allies along the way. Together with the trolls and tauren, the orcs put aside their old hatreds and united with two unlikely allies in order to halt a massive assault by the Burning Legion, led by the demon lord Archimonde. Together, orcs, humans, and night elves managed to put an end to Archimonde and bring a halt to the Legion's onslaught atop the peaks of Mount Hyjal.

WARCRAFT III: THE FROZEN THRONE

Although the united forces of Kalimdor were successful at ending the Burning Legion's assault, the Legion's once-loyal Scourge now stood on its own, still a threat in the Eastern Kingdoms. Arthas Menethil, now a death knight in the service of the Lich King, scoured the kingdom of Lordaeron, leaving behind a swath of death and devastation. Yet Arthas did not stand unopposed – the banshee Sylvanas Windrunner, a former high elf ranger-general, rebelled against the Lich King's control, forming a splinter faction of undead called the Forsaken.

On Kalimdor, the demon-tainted night elf Illidan Stormrage was contacted by the Burning Legion and given the task of taking out the Lich King, a journey that led him from Kalimdor to the Eastern Kingdoms and finally to the continent of Northrend, where he sought out the Lich King's throne in the frozen peaks of Icecrown, intent upon destroying the Lich King. Arthas rushed to his master's defense, defeating Illidan after a mighty battle that sent the servant of the Legion to Outland in shame. Triumphant, Arthas strode up the stairs of the Frozen Throne and embraced his dark destiny, placing the helm of the Lich King on his head and merging his spirit with that of his dark master.

WORLD OF WARCRAFT

World of Warcraft continued the story that began in the original RTS franchise. A critical success, the game has spawned several expansions over the past ten years, each with its own unique story to tell. Players actively take part in the story as heroes of Azeroth, choosing from a multitude of races and classes to take a triumphant role in the forces of the Alliance or Horde.

WORLD OF WARCRAFT

Ten years passed after the fall of Archimonde in Kalimdor, and the Horde, led by Warchief Thrall, expanded its ranks and embraced the Forsaken as allies. Yet they did not stand unopposed – the night elves, led by Malfurion Stormrage and Tyrande Whisperwind, joined the allied races of the Alliance. But the Alliance had its own struggles as well, as the human leader, King Varian Wrynn of Stormwind, suddenly and mysteriously disappeared. The kingdom of Stormwind faltered in his absence, due to the clever machinations and scheming of the black dragon Onyxia, disguised as a human noblewoman named Katrana Prestor. Meanwhile, her brother Nefarian presented a threat from the heights of Blackrock Spire. Although heroes sought to uncover Onyxia's deception, and defeat her brother as well, the dragons were far from the only threat they would face.

WORLD OF WARCRAFT

Deep within the sealed halls of Ahn'Qiraj, the dread Old God C'Thun stirred, its armies of qiraji soldiers bolstering its strength for an attack upon Azeroth itself. Although the Alliance and Horde triumphantly allied to battle these threats, the alliance was a tenuous one at best. Squabbles between the two factions were common, despite the efforts of Warchief Thrall and the human sorceress Jaina Proudmoore to forge a new era of peace and diplomacy.

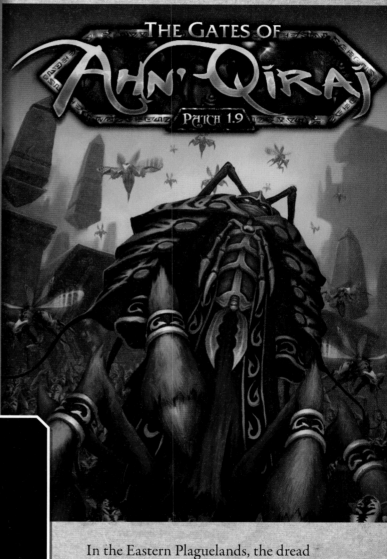

THE GATES OF Ahn'Qiraj

Patch 1.9

In the Eastern Plaguelands, the dread citadel Naxxramas unleashed a reign of terror led by Kel'Thuzad, the Lich King's loyal servant. Once again, both Alliance and Horde worked together to combat the threat. Although Kel'Thuzad and the Scourge were defeated, more trouble threatened to strike. Far to the south, the Dark Portal stirred once again, its gates opening to allow those heroes with enough courage to take the first few steps through into the shattered realm of Outland.

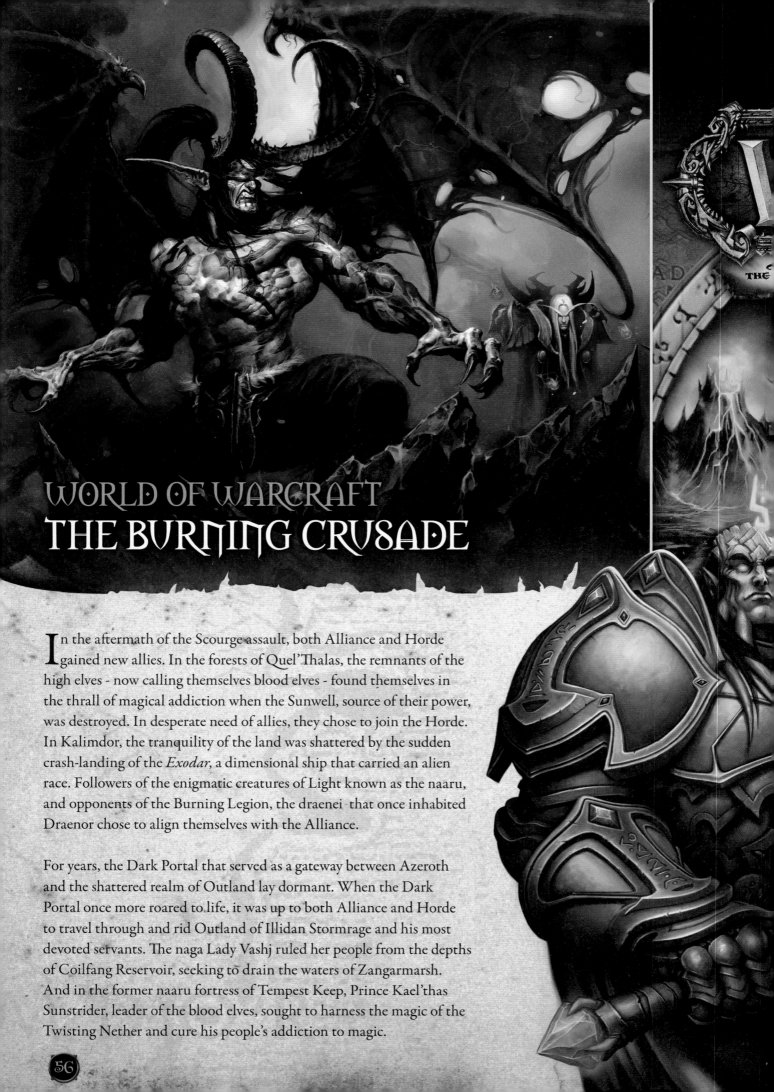

WORLD OF WARCRAFT
THE BURNING CRUSADE

In the aftermath of the Scourge assault, both Alliance and Horde gained new allies. In the forests of Quel'Thalas, the remnants of the high elves - now calling themselves blood elves - found themselves in the thrall of magical addiction when the Sunwell, source of their power, was destroyed. In desperate need of allies, they chose to join the Horde. In Kalimdor, the tranquility of the land was shattered by the sudden crash-landing of the *Exodar*, a dimensional ship that carried an alien race. Followers of the enigmatic creatures of Light known as the naaru, and opponents of the Burning Legion, the draenei that once inhabited Draenor chose to align themselves with the Alliance.

For years, the Dark Portal that served as a gateway between Azeroth and the shattered realm of Outland lay dormant. When the Dark Portal once more roared to life, it was up to both Alliance and Horde to travel through and rid Outland of Illidan Stormrage and his most devoted servants. The naga Lady Vashj ruled her people from the depths of Coilfang Reservoir, seeking to drain the waters of Zangarmarsh. And in the former naaru fortress of Tempest Keep, Prince Kael'thas Sunstrider, leader of the blood elves, sought to harness the magic of the Twisting Nether and cure his people's addiction to magic.

Azeroth thought their prince was seeking a cure, but he had descended into madness, allying himself not with Illidan Stormrage, but with Stormrage's former master – the demon lord Kil'jaeden. Kael'thas was not the only servant of Illidan to betray his master. Below the Black Temple, the elder sage Akama plotted against Illidan, seeking to reclaim the temple and restore it to its former glory. With the help of the night elf Maiev Shadowsong and a band of heroes, Illidan Stormrage was at last defeated.

Just when Outland's troubles had passed, peril chose to strike Azeroth. Kept alive through his defeat, Prince Kael'thas Sunstrider returned to the Isle of Quel'Danas to reignite the Sunwell, source of the blood elves' power, although his intent was not to reinvigorate his people. Instead, Kael'thas sought to use the Sunwell to summon his new master, Kil'jaeden, to Azeroth. Kael'thas met his end, and Kil'jaeden's plot was thwarted. But the Sunwell was not lost – the Prophet Velen, leader of the draenei, reignited the magical font using the heart of a fallen naaru. For a short time, violence between Alliance and Horde stilled – but any tentative thoughts of peace were about to be put to the test once more.

WORLD OF WARCRAFT
WRATH OF THE LICH KING

Although all was quiet after the Sunwell's purification, it was not to last long. The undead Scourge, led by the Lich King, launched an all-out assault against Azeroth, including both Stormwind City and Orgrimmar. Pressured to retaliate, Warchief Thrall dispatched a Horde force led by Overlord Garrosh Hellscream to Northrend. Meanwhile, King Varian Wrynn was at last returned to Stormwind, reclaiming his crown and sending a force of his own to Northrend, led by Highlord Bolvar Fordragon. While both factions were focused on the downfall of the Lich King, in most cases, they were not working side by side. Yet the Lich King was far from the only threat in Northrend. Dwarven explorer Brann Bronzebeard discovered the ancient titan fortress Ulduar, home to secrets untold and prison to a horrifying being of unfathomable evil -- the Old God Yogg-Saron. Left unchecked, Yogg-Saron's influence had

slowly spread across the entirety of Northrend. Heroes of both Alliance and Horde delved into the depths of the stronghold to put an end to Yogg-Saron, and to uncover what mysteries lay within.

Meanwhile, Highlord Tirion Fordring, head of the organization of holy soldiers known as the Argent Crusade, prepared to launch a final assault against the Lich King and his stronghold, Icecrown Citadel. Champions from both factions tested their mettle to prove they were worthy of taking part in the final assault by participating in a tournament of Fordring's design. Although the Scourge attempted to sabotage the tournament, Azeroth's heroes stood triumphant in the end, ready for what awaited them in the halls of the Lich King's fortress.

Both Alliance and Horde converged on Icecrown Citadel. From the Alliance, Lady Jaina Proudmoore sought to discover whether a part of her former lover Arthas Menethil still lived within the Lich King. The Banshee Queen, Sylvanas Windrunner, had a more straightforward task, to take out the Lich King and have her vengeance upon him at long last. Icecrown Citadel was successfully stormed, and the Lich King at last put to rest. But the moment of triumph was short-lived, as there must always be a Lich King. Highlord Bolvar Fordragon, thought dead to the plague, stepped forward to willingly take the helm of the Lich King as his own, and prevent the evils of the Scourge from rising again.

WORLD OF WARCRAFT
CATACLYSM

The effects of the Cataclysm brought new allies to both Alliance and Horde. The Alliance rescued the citizens of Gilneas, afflicted with a curse that caused them to transform into monstrous worgen. The Horde recruited the wily, scheming goblins of the Bilgewater Cartel.

The Northrend campaign was a success, although not without its losses. Alliance and Horde returned home in triumph, ready for a respite that was not to be. Elemental unrest swept across Azeroth, and in an effort to discover the cause, Warchief Thrall stepped down from the Horde, naming Garrosh Hellscream as warchief in his stead. The restless elements were a portent of horrors to come as Deathwing, the mad Dragon Aspect, burst forth from the elemental plane of Deepholm and ripped the world asunder in the process. Once freed, Deathwing began to gather powerful allies to his side. The Twilight's Hammer cult, Ragnaros the Firelord, and countless others worked to bring about the end of Azeroth – the Hour of Twilight. In the wake of the Cataclysm's devastation, the Zandalar tribe sought to reunite all the troll tribes in an attempt to rebuild their once-mighty empire. Vol'jin, chieftain of the Darkspear tribe (which allied with the Horde), stood alone against their plans, instead recruiting both his Horde allies and heroes of the Alliance to thwart the Zandalari onslaught.

WORLD OF WARCRAFT CATACLYSM

to stop him – the Dragon Soul. Lost in time, the artifact was retrieved by champions and brought to the present, delivered to the hands of Thrall (now called Go'el). With his assistance, the Aspects used the Dragon Soul to strike a blow that knocked Deathwing from the skies of Azeroth, tumbling into the Maelstrom at the heart of Azeroth's oceans. Yet it took their combined efforts and energies to bring about Deathwing's ultimate demise. Having expended their powers, the Dragon Aspects concluded that the continued protection of the world was now in the hands of Azeroth's heroes. The Age of Mortals had begun.

At the peaks of Mount Hyjal, chaos erupted when Ragnaros the Firelord and his elemental minions threatened to set the world ablaze. Although thought vanquished, Ragnaros continued to scheme from his home in the Firelands, and traitorous druids allied with the Firelord to assist with his fiery onslaught. In an effort to thwart another attack, Azeroth's heroes launched an assault on the Firelands. In that elemental plane, Ragnaros and his minions were at their strongest – yet the champions of Azeroth prevailed, with the help of Archdruid Malfurion Stormrage.

But even as Deathwing's allies fell, one by one, the Destroyer continued in his mad plans to end the world. In desperation, the Dragon Aspects sought the only artifact powerful enough

WORLD OF WARCRAFT
MISTS OF PANDARIA

With Deathwing's downfall secured, Warchief Garrosh Hellscream began a new campaign to strike at the Alliance and seize more territory for the Horde on Kalimdor. Using a mana bomb, he obliterated the human port town of Theramore, causing the tension between the two factions to erupt into all-out war. Later, a naval skirmish left both Alliance and Horde forces washed ashore on an island continent once thought mere legend: Pandaria.

This strange new land was rich with resources, and the Horde fought to establish footholds on it while the Alliance sought to combat their efforts. Both factions soon made contact and established alliances with the indigenous pandaren. Yet the bloody factional conflict resulted in the release of the sha, dark creatures born from negative emotion and thought. Together with the pandaren, both Alliance and Horde sought to disperse the dread enemy from Pandaria's shores, as well as fight ancient enemies of the pandaren – the mantid and the mogu.

Yet conflicts between the two factions continued to rise. The full force of Alliance and Horde armies arrived on Pandaria's shores, and Warchief Hellscream sought out the Divine Bell, an ancient mogu artifact that held the potential of imbuing Horde soldiers with unimaginable power. Hellscream's reckless actions held dire consequences for the Horde, including a violent outbreak against the Darkspear trolls, and the expulsion of the blood elves from the once-neutral city of Dalaran. Warchief Hellscream managed to claim the Divine Bell, but his efforts to use the artifact were thwarted by Alliance Prince Anduin Wrynn, who used the Harmonic Mallet to cancel the artifact's disastrous effects.

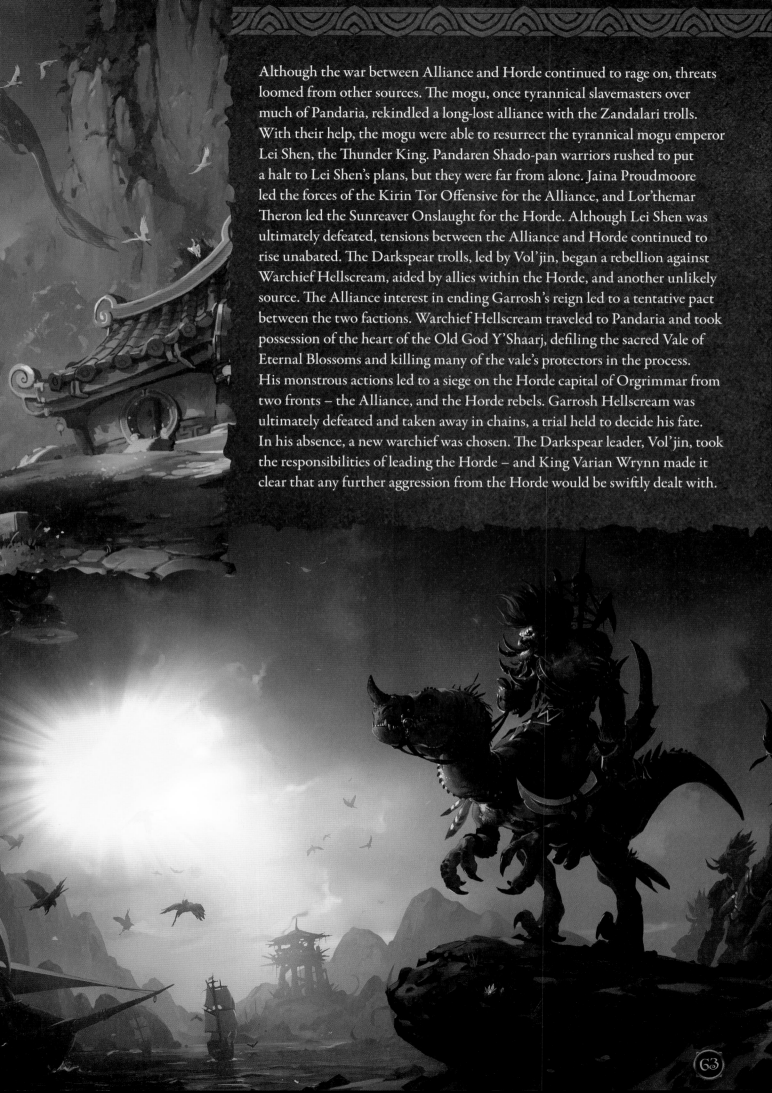

Although the war between Alliance and Horde continued to rage on, threats loomed from other sources. The mogu, once tyrannical slavemasters over much of Pandaria, rekindled a long-lost alliance with the Zandalari trolls. With their help, the mogu were able to resurrect the tyrannical mogu emperor Lei Shen, the Thunder King. Pandaren Shado-pan warriors rushed to put a halt to Lei Shen's plans, but they were far from alone. Jaina Proudmoore led the forces of the Kirin Tor Offensive for the Alliance, and Lor'themar Theron led the Sunreaver Onslaught for the Horde. Although Lei Shen was ultimately defeated, tensions between the Alliance and Horde continued to rise unabated. The Darkspear trolls, led by Vol'jin, began a rebellion against Warchief Hellscream, aided by allies within the Horde, and another unlikely source. The Alliance interest in ending Garrosh's reign led to a tentative pact between the two factions. Warchief Hellscream traveled to Pandaria and took possession of the heart of the Old God Y'Shaarj, defiling the sacred Vale of Eternal Blossoms and killing many of the vale's protectors in the process. His monstrous actions led to a siege on the Horde capital of Orgrimmar from two fronts – the Alliance, and the Horde rebels. Garrosh Hellscream was ultimately defeated and taken away in chains, a trial held to decide his fate. In his absence, a new warchief was chosen. The Darkspear leader, Vol'jin, took the responsibilities of leading the Horde – and King Varian Wrynn made it clear that any further aggression from the Horde would be swiftly dealt with.

WORLD OF WARCRAFT QUIZ

TEST OF LORE

Warcraft's history is a complicated one, involving a vast sea of faces and places on Azeroth and beyond. How well have you learned Azeroth's lessons? Answer these 20 true-or-false questions, then check your answers on page 77.

1

Sargeras possessed the human sorcerer Medivh.

TRUE FALSE

2

In order to stop Deathwing, the Dragon Aspects sought a powerful artifact called the Divine Bell.

TRUE FALSE

3

The draenei crash-landed on Azeroth in a dimensional ship called the *Arcatraz*.

TRUE FALSE

4

The mogu, ancient slavemasters of the pandaren race, rekindled a lost alliance with the Darkspear tribe of trolls.

TRUE FALSE

5

Warchief Thrall stepped down from leading the Horde, and named Garrosh Hellscream as warchief in his stead.

TRUE FALSE

6

The Lich King's stronghold is called Icecrown Citadel.

TRUE FALSE

7

The black dragon Onyxia disguised herself as a gnomish noblewoman named Katrana Prestor.

TRUE ☐ FALSE ☐

8

After the Second War, the orcs were placed in Alliance internment camps, and later liberated by Thrall.

TRUE ☐ FALSE ☐

9

The undead Scourge were unleashed on Azeroth by the Burning Legion.

TRUE ☐ FALSE ☐

10

The Alliance Conclave was stranded with no way home when Draenor shattered into Outland.

TRUE ☐ FALSE ☐

11

Prince Kael'thas Dawnstrider once led the blood elves, but eventually allied with the demon lord Kil'jaeden.

TRUE ☐ FALSE ☐

12

The Alliance forces in Northrend were led by Highlord Bolvar Fordragon.

TRUE ☐ FALSE ☐

13

The Zandalar tribe once sought to reunite all the troll tribes on Azeroth in an attempt to rebuild their empire.

TRUE ☐ FALSE ☐

14

The Shado are dark creatures born from negative emotion and thought, found on Pandaria.

TRUE ☐ FALSE ☐

15

The Old God Yogg-Saron was imprisoned in Ulduar, a titan fortress located in Northrend.

TRUE ☐ FALSE ☐

16

Lady Vashj sought to drain the waters of Zangarmarsh into her lair within Venomfang Reservoir.

TRUE ☐ FALSE ☐

17

During the Third War, both Alliance and Horde came together to defeat Kil'jaeden, bringing a halt to the Legion's onslaught on Mount Hyjal.

TRUE ☐ FALSE ☐

18

The human survivors of the First War fled across the Great Sea after Stormwind's destruction, led by Anduin Wrynn.

TRUE ☐ FALSE ☐

19

To construct the Dark Portal between Azeroth and Draenor, the sorcerer Medivh worked with an orc warlock named Gul'dan.

TRUE ☐ FALSE ☐

20

The Banshee Queen, Sylvanas Windrunner, was once a high elf ranger-general.

TRUE ☐ FALSE ☐

YOUR SCORE

out of 20

65

PROPHET'S WISDOM

Use the images below to reveal the Prophet Velen's hidden message on the opposite page.

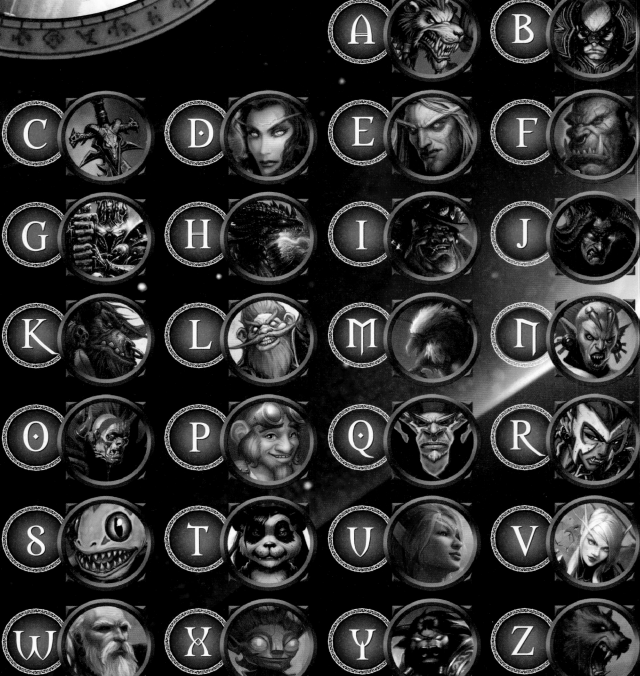

A B C D E F G H I J K L M N O P Q R S T U V W X Y Z

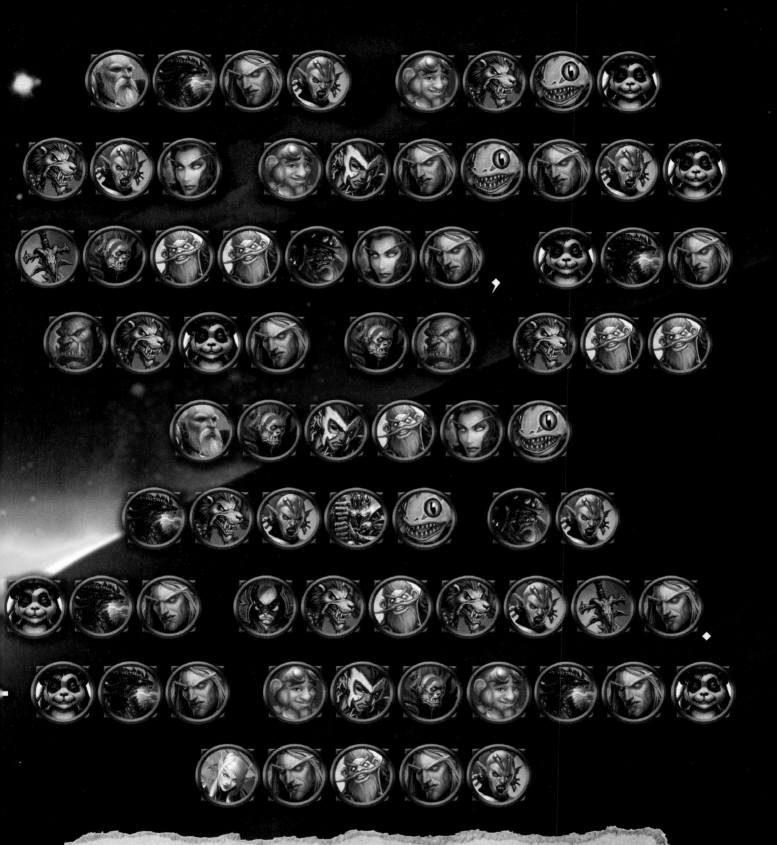

Write the secret message here:

WORLD OF WARCRAFT
WARLORDS OF DRAENOR

Although apprehended for the crimes and atrocities he committed, Garrosh Hellscream escaped his fate, aided by a mysterious ally. While on trial at the Temple of the White Tiger, Garrosh managed to flee by doing the unthinkable - traversing time itself to journey to an alternate version of Draenor, a savage world fraught with conflict.

Given the unique opportunity to change fate, Garrosh seized the chance to stop the orc clans from succumbing to the Burning Legion's corruption and instead forged a new Horde of iron, rather than fel blood. This new Iron Horde sought to trample Draenor beneath the might of terrifying war machines, before making a move on Azeroth itself. On Azeroth, the Dark Portal, once thought linked solely to the world of Outland, exploded in activity as the orcs linked their altered version of Draenor to Azeroth.

The tides of war loomed once more, as an echo of the First War once again threatened to overrun the fragile world ... this time, with a far stronger, savage, deadly legion – the terrifying might of the Iron Horde. The Iron Horde's version of Draenor bore only the slightest resemblance to the shattered world of Outland. Untouched by the Burning Legion's corruption, the land teemed with deadly beauty once thought lost to the ravages of history. Draenei settlements and cities still remained whole and pure, but orcish assaults were a constant threat to the draenei race. Garrosh Hellscream may have changed the fates of the orc clans, but he did little to discourage the hatreds between orc and draenei that had boiled over into all-out war. Yet though the draenei may have been ravaged by war, they were far from defeated.

HEROES AND VILLAINS OF DRAENOR

KARGATH BLADEFIST

Clan: Shattered Hand
Territory: Spires of Arak

Kargath leads the Shattered Hand, a vicious clan of hate-filled sadists. In tribute and to emulate their chieftain, members of the Shattered Hand have followed his example of body modification, replacing one of their hands with brutal weaponry.

BLACKHAND

Clan: Blackrock
Territory: Gorgrond

Tactically brilliant and power-mad, Blackhand is a notoriously cruel weaponmaster. Under his leadership, the Blackrock clan utilizes slaves to forge terrifying siege engines for the Iron Horde.

Clan: Bleeding Hollow
Territory: Tanaan Jungle

Kilrogg "Deadeye" saw his own death during a vision quest, tearing his left eyeball from his skull in a brutal show of symbolism. The Bleeding Hollow clan strikes down their enemies with vicious, berserk fury, slathering their weapons in hallucinogenic venom and stalking their prey from the treetops.

KILROGG

GUL'DAN

Clan: Shadowmoon
Territory: Shadowmoon Valley

Although contemplative and forward-thinking, Ner'zhul's vision of the future has been eclipsed by the manipulations of his apprentice, Gul'dan. The Shadowmoon may look reverently to the stars for guidance, but the reality of the rising Iron Horde remains a looming future impossible to ignore.

NER'ZHUL

Territory: Shadowmoon Valley

Gul'dan was once apprentice to Ner'zhul. Pitted against his former mentor and indebted to a demonic lord, Gul'dan is now one of a few fel orcs on Draenor.

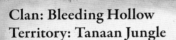

DUROTAN

Clan: Frostwolf
Territory: Frostfire Ridge

Loyal and wise in the eyes of his allies, terrifying in the eyes of his enemies, Durotan leads the Frostwolf clan from the harsh and hostile reaches of Frostfire Ridge. Durotan and his people rejected the Iron Horde's call for orcish unity, instead focusing on their own survival in the biting cold of the frozen north.

GROMMASH

Faction: Alliance

Khadgar was once apprentice to the Guardian Medivh, until he helped defeat his master and destroy the Dark Portal created to summon the orcs to Azeroth. Although cursed with frailty and age, Khadgar remains an exemplar for the Alliance, leading counterattacks against the Burning Legion and all who would threaten Azeroth with annihilation.

KHADGAR

Clan: Warsong
Territory: Nagrand

Grommash Hellscream leads the Warsong clan, a nomadic group of dead-eyed archers and bellowing raiders. Gathering at the vanguard of the Iron Horde, the Warsongs raze their enemies' lands and homes to embers, then stamp the dying embers into ash.

MARAAD

VELEN

Faction: Alliance

The ancient leader of the draenei, the Prophet Velen has spent millennia weighing and recording the futures he foresees so that creation itself does not fall. Although Velen's guidance saved his people during the exodus of their homeworld, Argus, his wisdom is in question after the arrival of the Iron Horde on Draenor.

Faction: Alliance

A wandering warrior of faith, Vindicator Maraad is a bastion of Light in draenei society. After the campaign in Northrend, Maraad began instructing other races of the Alliance in the ways of the Light. Yet years of exposure to the perils of Azeroth have left the vindicator prone to action above meditation, willing and ready to strike where others may tarry.

WORDS OF WARLORDS

Draenor is full of unique people and places. Can you find all the words listed below?

- [ ] KARGATH
- [ ] BLACKHAND
- [ ] KILROGG
- [ ] SHADOWMOON
- [ ] GARROSH
- [ ] STORMREAVER
- [ ] WARSONG
- [ ] NAGRAND
- [ ] FROSTWOLF
- [ ] PORTAL
- [ ] KHADGAR
- [ ] MARAAD
- [ ] DRAENEI
- [ ] PROPHET
- [ ] SPIRES
- [ ] HELLSCREAM
- [ ] DUROTAN
- [ ] HORDE
- [ ] IRON
- [ ] FROSTFIRE
- [ ] GORGROND
- [ ] ARAK
- [ ] SHATTERED
- [ ] TANAAN
- [ ] ALLIANCE

```
F T S M A A B U L T X F P L L U H M P G
R L U P O O U V F R T J R A G J Z V B G
O O E P I S T A Q S M B T L J L A G C X
S U T C P R Z A H T Q R P C Y C N V T B
T T D D N H E A F H O E A S B G U X M N
F F D Q V A T S P P B L A C K H A N D A
I S R S L T I J O V Q K Y M H C K Z P G
R S U O E A Y L N L I M V Z O N V R N R
E V K R S V U F L N O R I A R C O H L A
Q U E H K T Z L S A O R C P J Z M Z S N
P D N N W F W I G R Y A T P D T Y D K D
L O A J P A I O N I E N E A R D Z S L E
A S T L H I R P L F M W F U Q E D V J M
W V O G T R E S L F H Z D G F S Y B K N
K Y R A A F V N O O F H F X R F S K A N
R T U X G Y H H R N S U L A B F H U F O
B E D R R L L D U H G E R G W A T B O O
E O V U A C E M G C J R Z D D D A R Q M
S V T A K G A R R O S H M G U E N V X W
D K X N E H T Z V A W A A Z Z E A U G O
E T A B F R D H R O E R S C R P A U G D
N C E R S T M D V R S F G B Q N A G Q A
D F D H A C I R C W N B K B Y F O Z N H
I U F E P K S S O B X T J H W R F H D S
X M F B H O L F O T R Q W X L D C G U O
U F V W R L R K C T S N I Q W Y P H N N
L T U I E P B P B F B K X S U X Q N I
R L E H O N J D R H D C I E Y H E T L M
D N O R G R O G L L F Z Z Z E R N Q M V
Z Z T P F P C H C I Z L M A R A A D N U
```

TRIVIA CHALLENGE

Are you confident in your knowledge of Azeroth and beyond? Do you think you know everything there is to know? Take the Lorewalkers' trivia challenge to test just how well you know the World of Warcraft!

1

Alleria, Sylvanas, and Vereesa are all members of what high elven family?

2

What is the name of the pandaren isle atop the turtle Shen-zin Su?

3

Garrosh Hellscream used a mana bomb to destroy which Alliance city?

4

The proto-dragon Galakrond's final resting place is located in which Northrend zone?

5

Who is the elemental lord of fire?

6

Which prophet leads the draenei people?

7
What is the historic capital city of the Bronzebeard dwarves?

8
Which Dragon Aspect leads the red dragonflight?

9
What is the name of Grommash Hellscream's famous axe?

10
The yaungol can be found on which continent of Azeroth?

11
Nightsabers are the racial mount of which race?

12
What is the name of Cairne Bloodhoof's son?

13
Gnomes elect their leader into the position of high tinker. Who currently holds this position?

14
A'dal is a member of which race?

15
The Thunder King is a member of which Pandaren race?

16
Who is the regent lord of Silvermoon City?

17
Who is the Black Prince, descendant of Deathwing?

18
What is the name of Grommash Hellscream's son?

19
Which orc was responsible for opening numerous portals on Draenor and shattering the orc homeworld?

20
The draenei are exiled members of a powerful race that was corrupted by Sargeras. What is the original name of that race?

YOUR SCORE

out of 20

ANSWERS

14–15 FACTION CROSSWORD

Across/Down answers:

THRALL, HAMMERS, ANCESTRAL, QEL'THALAS, TIGER, CLOUDSINGER, GREYMANE, BANSHEE, TECHNOLOGICAL, BLOODHOOF, VARIAN, KALDOREI, DARKSPEAR, THAURISSAN, BILGEWATER, FORSAKEN, GREHZIN, STORMRAGE, MEKKATORQUE, LOR'THEMAR, GALLYWIX, TYRANDE, ALLIANCE, PROPHET, KEZAN, GILNEAS, THIRD, WANDERING, DRAENOR, HORDE, VOL'JIN

24–25
CAPITAL MATCH-UP

DWARF – IRONFORGE
ORC – ORGRIMMAR
FORSAKEN – UNDERCITY
BLOOD ELF – SILVERMOON CITY
HUMAN – STORMWIND
TAUREN – THUNDER BLUFF
WORGEN – GILNEAS
DRAENEI – EXODAR

38–39
THE EMPEROR'S WAY

TEST OF LORE

1. TRUE	2. FALSE
3. FALSE	4. FALSE
5. TRUE	6. TRUE
7. FALSE	8. TRUE
9. TRUE	10. FALSE
11. FALSE	12. TRUE
13. TRUE	14. FALSE
15. TRUE	16. FALSE
17. FALSE	18. FALSE
19. TRUE	20. TRUE

WORDS OF WARLORDS

```
F T S M A A B U L T X F P R A G U H M P G
R L U P O O U V F R T J R A G J Z V B G
O O E P I S T A Q S M B T L J L A G C X
S U T C P R Z A H T O R P C Y C N V T B
T T D D N H E A F H O E A S B G U X M N
F F D Q V A T S P P B L A C K H A N D A
I S R S L T I J O V Q K Y M H C K Z P G
R S U O E A Y L N L I M V Z O N V R N R
E V K S V U F L N O R I A R C O H L A
Q U E H K T Z L S A O R C P J Z M Z S N
P D N N W F W I G R Y A T P D T Y D K
L O A J P A I O N I E N E A R D Z S L E
A S T L H I R P L F M W F U Q E D V J M
W V O G T R E S L F H Z D G F S Y B K N
K Y R A A F V N O O F H F X R F S K A N
R T U X G Y H H R N S U L A B F W T U O
B E D R R L L D U H G T W A T B O O
E O V U A C E M G C J R Z D D Q A R Q M
S V T A K G A R R O S H M G A U N X W
D K X N E H T Z V A W A A Z S E A U G O
E T A B F R D H R Q E R S C R P A U G D
N C E R S T M D V R S F G B Q R G N Q A
D F D H A C I R C W N B K B Y E O Z N H
I U F E P K S S O B X T J H W R F H D S
X M F B H O L F O T R Q W X L D C G U O
U F V W R L R K C T S G N I Q W Y P H N
L T U L E P B P B F B P K X S U X Q N I
R L E H O N J D R H D C I E Y H E T L M
D N O R G R O G L L F Z Z Z E R N Q M V
Z Z T P F P C H C I Z L M A R A A D N U
```

66–67
PROPHET'S WISDOM

WHEN PAST AND PRESENT COLLIDE, THE FATE OF ALL WORLDS HANGS IN THE BALANCE.

– THE PROPHET VELEN

74–75
TRIVIA CHALLENGE

1. WINDRUNNER
2. WANDERING ISLE
3. THERAMORE ISLE
4. DRAGONBLIGHT
5. RAGNAROS THE FIRELORD
6. VELEN
7. IRONFORGE
8. ALEXSTRASZA
9. GOREHOWL
10. PANDARIA
11. NIGHT ELVES
12. BAINE
13. GELBIN MEKKATORQUE
14. THE NAARU
15. THE MOGU
16. LOR'THEMAR THERON
17. WRATHION
18. GARROSH
19. NER'ZHUL
20. THE EREDAR

77